Sauce Cookbook:

50 The Best Sauce Recipes for Every Day

Table of Contents:

Almond and orange sauce

Cowberry sauce

Cherry-wine sauce

Plum sweet sauce

Peach sauce

Apricot and cognac sauce

Milk-almond sauce

Vanilla sauce

Vanilla sauce with lemon zest

Vanilla-chocolate sauce

Vanilla sauce with nuts

Chocolate and milk sauce

Chocolate-rum sauce

Chocolate sauce with hazelnuts

Chocolate-coffee sauce

Introduction

The sauce is not a dish, sauce – instrument, once one of the most important chefs, is now rarely used, but still retaining its meaning "Creator" or "controller" of the taste of the dish. The French say: the architect covers up my mistakes façade, chef sauce, doctor earth. "Sauce" literally means "salty", "salty". This book will make your usual meals a tasty and unusual and will surprise your family!

Sauce "Carbonara"

ngredients:

- 300 g smoked ham
- 200 ml cream
- 4 egg yolks
- 2 cloves of garlic
- 30 ml of olive oil
- Pepper, salt to taste

Preparation:

Ham cut into small cubes. Garlic clean, wash, finely chopped. In the saucepan, heat up the olive oil, put the garlic, cook for 1 minute. Then add the ham and cook or 2-3 minutes, stirring occasionally.

Then, with constant stirring, add the cream, whipped with yolks, warm until thick do not boil so that the yolks do not curl up). Remove the sauce from the fire, season with pepper and salt, serve with pasta and spaghetti.

Garlic sauce with greens

Ingredients:
- 3 cloves of garlic
- 50 ml of olive oil
- 10 grams of green basil, oregano and thyme
- Pepper, salt

Preparation:
Garlic clean, wash, finely chopped. Wash green, dry, chop. Olive oil warm in a saucepan, add the garlic and cook over low heat until golden brown (about 3 minutes). Then take the garlic with a whisk, put greens in the saucepan, add salt pepper, mix and remove from heat. Sauce to serve to pasta immediately after cooking.

Creamy sauce with mushrooms and minced meat

Ingredients:

- 200 g minced meat
- 150 g of mushrooms (white or champignons)
- 300 ml cream
- 1 onion
- 1-2 cloves of garlic
- 50 ml of olive oil
- Pepper, salt

Preparation:

Onion and garlic peeled, washed, finely chopped. Mushrooms pick, rinse, cut into small pieces. In the frying pan, heat olive oil, put onion and garlic, fry for 2-3 minutes, then add the forcemeat and mushrooms, add salt, pepper, stir and fry for 5-7 minutes. After that, add the cream, bring the sauce to a boil over low heat with constant stirring. Serve the sauce for small pasta.

Creamy sauce with bacon and greens

Ingredients:
- 150 g of bacon
- 300 ml cream
- 1 onion
- 1-2 cloves of garlic
- 1 small pod of red hot pepper
- 50 ml of olive oil
- Parsley and basil greens
- Pepper, salt

Preparation:
Onion and garlic peeled, washed, finely chopped. Sharp pepper, remove the stem and seeds, cut into strips. Greens of parsley and basil are washed, dried and chopped. Bacon cut into small pieces. In a frying pan, heat olive oil, put onion and garlic, fry for 2-3 minutes, then add bacon and hot pepper, stir and fry another 1-2 minutes.

After that, add the cream, bring the sauce to a boil over low heat with constant stirring, season with salt and pepper. Remove from heat, add parsley and basil greens, stir and remove the hay. Serve the sauce for pasta.

Creamy sauce with smoked salmon

Ingredients:
- 400 ml cream
- 200 g smoked salmon fillet
- 1 onion
- 2 cloves of garlic
- 50 ml of olive oil
- 1 teaspoon of starch
- Dill, pepper, salt

Preparation:
Onion and garlic peeled, washed, finely chopped. Dill dry, chop. Cut salmon fillets in small cubes. Put onion and garlic in a frying pan with preheated olive oil, fry until they become transparent. Pour the cream, add the starch, pepper and salt, bring to a boil over low heat with constant stirring. Add the pieces of fish and dill to the sauce, stir and remove from heat. Serve the sauce with spaghetti, linguini.

Spicy creamy sauce with shrimps

Ingredients:
- 400 ml cream
- 200 g of peeled shrimp
- 1 onion
- 2 cloves of garlic
- 1 pod of red hot pepper
- 50 ml of olive oil
- 1 teaspoon of starch
- Parsley and thyme, ground paprika, salt

Preparation:
Onion and garlic peeled, washed, finely chopped. Sharp pepper, remove the stem and seeds, cut into strips. Green parsley and thyme, wash, dry, chop. Beat the garlic and garlic in a frying pan with the olive oil heated, fry until they become transparent. Add shrimp and hot pepper, fry for 2-3 minutes. Then pour the cream, add the starch, paprika and salt, bring to a boil over low heat with constant stirring. Add the greens to the sauce, stir and remove from heat. Serve the sauce with spaghetti, linguini.

Bolognese classic sauce

ngredients:

- 700 g ground beef
- 800 g of canned tomatoes without peel
- 1 onion
- 1 carrot
- 1 stalk of celery
- 60 ml of olive oil
- 60 ml of dry red wine
- 60 ml cream
- Ground nutmeg
- Pepper, salt

Preparation:

Carrots and onion peel, wash, chop. Celery should be washed and cut into small pieces. Canned tomatoes cut into small pieces. Olive oil warmed up in a frying pan, put carrots, onions and celery, fry for 5-7 minutes, stirring occasionally. Put on the frying pan minced meat, mix thoroughly and fry for another 5-7 minutes. After that add tomatoes, wine, salt and spices, bring to a boil with stirring and simmer on low heat for 45-60 minutes, stirring occasionally. At the end of the cooking, add the cream to the sauce, heat on medium heat for 1-2 minutes, remove from heat. Serve the sauce with spaghetti, tagliatelle.

Sauce Bolognese with porcini mushrooms and ham

Ingredients:
- 700 grams of mixed stuffing (pork, beef)
- 800 g of canned tomatoes without peel
- 200 g of ceps
- 100 g smoked ham
- 1 onion
- 1 carrot
- 1 stalk of celery
- 60 ml of olive oil
- 60 ml of dry red wine
- 60 ml cream
- Ground nutmeg
- Pepper, salt

Preparation:
Carrots and onion peel, wash, chop. Celery should be washed and cut into small pieces. Canned tomatoes cut into small pieces. White mushrooms to sort, rinse, cu into slices. Ham cut into small cubes. Olive oil warmed up in a frying pan, put carrots, onions and celery, fry for 5-7 minutes, stirring occasionally. Put on the frying pan minced meat, mix thoroughly and fry for another 5-7 minutes. Put the mushrooms on the pan, fry for another 2-3 minutes.

Then add ham, tomatoes, wine, salt and spices, bring to a boil with stirring and simmer on low heat for 45-60 minutes, stirring occasionally. At the end of the cooking, add the cream to the sauce, heat on medium heat for 1-2 minutes, remove from heat.

Serve the sauce with spaghetti, tagliatelle.

Sauce Bolognese from chicken mince with cherry and greens

Ingredients:

- 600 g of chicken ground meat
- 800 grams of cherry
- 100 ml of tomato juice
- 1 onion
- 1 carrot
- 1 stalk of celery
- 60 ml of olive oil
- 60 ml of dry red wine
- 60 ml cream
- Green thyme and parsley
- Ground nutmeg
- Pepper, salt

Preparation:

Carrots and onion peel, wash, chop. Celery should be washed and cut into small pieces. Cherry tomatoes, wash with boiling water, peel and cut into halves. Green thyme and parsley to wash, dry and finely chop. Olive oil warmed up in a frying pan, put carrots, onions and celery, fry for 5-7 minutes, stirring occasionally. Put the chicken forcemeat into the pan, mix thoroughly and fry for another 5-7 minutes. After that add tomatoes, tomato juice, wine, salt and spices, bring to a boil, stirring, and simmer on low heat for 45-60 minutes, stirring occasionally. At the end of the cooking, add the cream to the sauce, heat on medium heat for 1-2 minutes, remove from heat. Serve the sauce with pasta, spaghetti, linguine.

Sauce with mushrooms and seafood

Ingredients:
- 400 ml of creamy cream
- 200 g of white mushrooms or champignons
- 100 g of peeled mussels
- 100 g of peeled shrimp
- 1 onion
- 2 cloves of garlic
- 50 ml of olive oil
- 1 teaspoon of starch
- Parsley, ground paprika, salt

Preparation:
Onion and garlic peeled, washed, finely chopped. Mushrooms pick, rinse, cut into thin slices. Clean parsley, drain, chop. Put onion and garlic in a frying pan with preheated olive oil, fry until they become transparent. Add the mushrooms, stir and fry for 4-5 minutes. Then add the defrosted seafood, warm, pour in the cream, add the starch, paprika and salt, bring to a boil over low heat with constant stirring. Add parsley to the sauce, stir and remove from heat. Serve the sauce with spaghetti. It can also be used to make casseroles from small pasta.

Tomato sauce with champignons and lemon juice

Ingredients:
- 300 g basic red sauce
- 75 g of tomato puree
- 75 g of champignons
- 50 ml of dry white wine
- 50 ml of lemon juice
- 1 small onion
- 30 ml of olive oil
- Parsley and tarragon, pepper, salt

Preparation:
Peel onion, wash, finely chopped. Parsley and tarragon grease, chop. Champignons washed, cut into small pieces. Olive oil to warm up in a frying pan, to lay out mushrooms, an onion, to fry, constantly stirring, 5-7 minutes. Red the main sauce slightly warmed, put in it fried onions and mushrooms, add tomato puree, lemon juice and white wine. Cook, stirring, on low heat for 5-7 minutes, then add greens, salt and pepper. Again bring the sauce to a boil and remove from heat. This sauce is recommended to be served to small pasta.

Vegetable sauce for spaghetti

Ingredients:
- 2 onions
- 2 pods of bell pepper
- 1 carrot
- 2 stalks of celery
- 2-3 cloves of garlic
- 4 tomatoes
- 60 ml of olive oil
- White and black ground pepper, salt

Preparation:
Onions, carrots and garlic are cleaned, washed, finely chopped. Wash Bulgarian pepper, remove stems and seeds, chop finely. Celery should be washed and cut into small pieces. Wash tomatoes, turn over with boiling water, peel and cut into small pieces. In the frying pan, heat olive oil, put onion and garlic, fry for 1-2 minutes. Then add carrot, bell pepper and celery, fry another 5 minutes over medium heat, stirring occasionally. Put in the pan tomatoes, salt, pepper, cook under the lid on low heat for 10 minutes. This sauce can be served both hot and cold.

Apple sauce with cinnamon and cloves

ngredients:

- 500 g of apples
- 200 g of sugar or powdered sugar
- 1 lemon
- 15 g of starch
- Ground cinnamon, ground cloves

reparation:

pples wash, peel, remove the core, coarsely chop. Wash lemon, peel the grated est, squeeze the juice. Apple peel pour 200 ml of water, add sugar or powdered ugar, bring to a boil, cook for 10 minutes, drain. Put into the broth pieces of pples, cook until soft, 1-2 minutes before the readiness to add lemon juice, lemon est, cinnamon and cloves. Wipe the apples through a fine sieve, mix with the roth, add the starch and cook on low heat until thickened with constant stirring. erve sauce in hot or cold form to sweet casseroles, porridges, puddings.

Apple-orange sauce

Ingredients:
- 500 g of apples
- 2 oranges
- 200 g of sugar or powdered sugar
- 50 ml of lemon juice
- 15 g of starch
- 1 packet of vanilla sugar
- 30 ml of orange liqueur
- Ground cinnamon

Preparation:
Apples wash, peel, remove the core, coarsely chop. Oranges should be washed, grated with peel, seeds removed. Apple peel pour 200 ml of water, add sugar or powdered sugar, bring to a boil, cook for 10 minutes, drain. Put into the broth pieces of apples, cook until soft, 1-2 minutes before the readiness to add lemon juice and cinnamon. Wipe the apples through a sieve, mix with broth and oranges add vanilla sugar and starch, bring to a boil over low heat with constant stirring. Remove from heat, cool, add orange liqueur, stir. Serve sauce with sweet casseroles, porridges, puddings.

Apple-cream sauce

Ingredients:
- 500 g of apples
- 200 ml cream
- 200 g of sugar or powdered sugar
- 30 ml of lemon juice
- 15 g of starch
- 1 packet of vanilla sugar
- 1 teaspoon grated orange peel

Preparation:
Apples wash, remove the core, cut into large pieces, pour 200 ml of water, add lemon juice, sugar or sugar powder, bring to a boil, cook until soft, wipe through a sieve. In the resulting mashed potatoes add starch, diluted in a small amount of cold water, vanilla sugar and orange peel. Bring to a boil over low heat, cook with constant stirring until thickened, cool. Add chilled cream, lightly whisk. Serve the dessert with fresh and canned fruit and berries.

Dried apples sauce

Ingredients:
- 300 g of dried apples
- 150 g of sugar
- 1 teaspoon orange peel
- 1 teaspoon lemon zest
- 1 teaspoon of starch
- 1 packet of vanilla sugar
- Ground cinnamon, ground cardamom

Preparation:
Apples thoroughly wash, pour 400 ml of water, add sugar and cook over low heat under the lid for 15-20 minutes. Wipe the apples through a sieve, add a decoction, vanilla sugar, orange and lemon zest, cinnamon, cardamom and starch, diluted in a small amount of cold water. With constant stirring, bring the sauce to a boil, chill. Serve with pancakes, fritters, casseroles from cereals and pasta.

Strawberry sauce with orange liqueur

Ingredients:
- 500 g strawberries
- 500 g of sugar
- 1 teaspoon strawberry liquor
- 1 teaspoon orange liqueur

Preparation:
Strawberry to sort out, remove stems and sepals, fill it with sugar and leave for 2-3 hours. Add 200 ml of water, bring to a boil and cook over low heat for 15 minutes, periodically removing the resulting foam. At the end of cooking add the orange and strawberry liqueurs, gently mix and remove from heat. Serve the sauce in hot or cold form to pancakes, fritters, puddings, ice cream.

Strawberry sauce with vanilla sugar

Ingredients:
- 700 g strawberries
- 200 g of sugar
- 1 packet of vanilla sugar
- 1 teaspoon of starch

Preparation:
Strawberry to sort out, remove stems and sepals, rub through a sieve. In the resulting puree add sugar and vanilla sugar, leave for 2-3 hours, then mix until the sugar dissolves completely.

Put the container with mashed potatoes on a weak fire, add the starch diluted in a small amount of cold water, bring to a boil with constant stirring, cool. Serve sauce with fresh and canned fruit salads, pancakes, fritters, casseroles.

Raspberry sauce with spices

Ingredients:

- 500 g of raspberry
- 500 g of sugar
- 1 teaspoon cognac
- 1 teaspoon orange peel
- Ground cinnamon
- Ground cloves
- Ground cardamom
- Ground buckwheat

Preparation:

Raspberry to sort out, remove stems and sepals, fill with sugar and leave for 2-3 hours. Then merge the resulting juice, the berries are wiped through a sieve. Add raspberry puree with juice, add orange zest, cinnamon, cloves, coriander and cardamom, bring to a boil with constant stirring. Remove the formed foam, add cognac, mix and remove from heat. Serve the sauce with desserts.

Cottage cheese sauce with forest berries

Ingredients:
- 100 g of fat cottage cheese
- 250 ml of milk
- 50 grams of blackberry
- 50 g of raspberry
- 50 g of blueberries
- 40 g of sugar

Preparation:
To make a curd cheese sauce, carefully curd the cheese with a wooden spoon, add sugar and milk, mix. Berries of blackberries, raspberries and blueberries to sort, wash, dry and dry through a sieve. The resulting juice is mixed with the curd sauce and beat until a uniform mass is formed. Serve the sauce with fruit salads.

Cottage cheese sauce with strawberries

Ingredients:
- 100 g of fat cottage cheese
- 250 ml of milk
- 150 g strawberries
- 40 g of sugar
- 1 packet of vanilla sugar

Preparation:
To make a curd cheese sauce, carefully curd the cheese with a wooden spoon, add sugar and milk, mix. Strawberry berries sort out, remove stems and sepals, wash, dry and dry through a sieve. The resulting juice is mixed with the curd sauce, add the vanilla sugar and beat with a mixer until a homogeneous mass is formed. Serve sauce with fruit salads, pasta.

Cottage cheese sauce with raspberries and mint

Ingredients:
- 100 g of fat cottage cheese
- 250 ml of milk
- 250 g of raspberry
- 40 g of sugar
- 1 packet of vanilla sugar
- 2-3 sprigs of mint

Preparation:
Mint wash, dry, finely chop. To make a curd cheese sauce, carefully curd the cheese with a wooden spoon, add sugar and milk, mix. Berries of raspberries to sort, remove stems and sepals, wash, dry and dry through a sieve. The resulting puree is mixed with the curd sauce and beat until a uniform mass is formed. Then add the vanilla sugar and mint, mix. Serve the sauce with salads and fresh fruit desserts.

Sauce from yogurt with vanilla

Ingredients:
- 200 ml of natural yogurt
- 200 ml of creamy cream
- 1 vanilla pod
- 100 g of powdered sugar

Preparation:
From the vanilla pod, remove the pulp, mix it with yogurt and cream. Add the powdered sugar, lightly whip with a whisk. Serve the sauce with chilled fruit salads, pancakes, puddings.

Yoghurt sauce with cherries

Ingredients:
- 400 ml of natural yogurt
- 250 g of sweet cherry
- 100 g of powdered sugar
- 1 packet of vanilla sugar

Preparation:
Cherries wash, remove stems and bones, cut into small pieces. Mix the yogurt with the sugar powder and vanilla sugar, whisk a little. Before serving, add to the resulting sauce pieces of sweet cherry and mix.

Creamy sauce with raspberries

ngredients:

- 300 ml fat cream
- 300 g of raspberry
- 100 g of powdered sugar
- 1 packet of vanilla sugar
- 1 teaspoon grated orange peel

reparation:

Berries of raspberries to sort, remove stems and sepals, wash, dry and dry through sieve (a few berries postponed). The resulting puree mixed with chilled cream nd powdered sugar, lightly whisk. Add vanilla sugar, orange zest and remaining aspberries to the sauce, gently mix. Serve the sauce with fritters, pancakes, asseroles.

Creamy sauce with blackberries and strawberries

Ingredients:
- 300 ml fat cream
- 100 grams of blackberry
- 200 g strawberries
- 100 g of powdered sugar
- 1 packet of vanilla sugar
- 1 teaspoon grated lemon zest
- 4-5 leaves of mint

Preparation:
Mint wash, dry, thinly cut. Berries of blackberries and strawberries sort out, remove stems and sepals, wash, dry and dry through a sieve (several berries postponed). The resulting puree mixed with chilled cream and powdered sugar lightly whisk. Add vanilla sugar, peppermint, lemon zest, vanilla berries, small pieces of strawberries into the sauce, and gently mix. Serve the sauce with fruit salads, casseroles and pasta.

Sour cream sauce with strawberries and lemon

Ingredients:
- 600 g sour cream
- 300 g of strawberry
- 1 lemon
- 100 ml of Madeira
- 100 g of powdered sugar
- Ground nutmeg

Preparation:
Remove strawberries, remove stems and sepals, rub through a sieve. Wash lemon, grate the zest on a small grater, squeeze the juice. Strawberry puree mixed with lemon juice and Madeira, add the powdered sugar, lemon zest and nutmeg, mix. Then add sour cream and whisk with a whisk until a uniform mass is formed. Serve the sauce with fresh fruit salads.

Sour cream sauce with apples and cinnamon

Ingredients:
- 600 g sour cream
- 2-3 sweet apples
- 100 g of powdered sugar
- 1 teaspoon grated orange peel
- Ground cinnamon

Preparation:
Apples should be washed, peeled, removed and grated on a fine grater. Add the powdered sugar, mix, bring to a boil over low heat, add the orange peel and cinnamon, stir to bring to a boil over low heat, add the orange peel and cinnamon mix and chill. Mix apple puree with sour cream, beat whisk until a homogeneous mass is formed. Serve the sauce with pancakes, fritters, puddings and casseroles.

Blackcurrant sauce with brandy

Ingredients:

- 800 g black currant
- 350 g of sugar
- 50 ml brandy
- 1 teaspoon grated lemon zest
- 1 packet of vanilla sugar
- 1 teaspoon of starch

Preparation:

Black currant to sort, wash, add sugar and 100 ml of water, bring to a boil and cook on low heat with constant stirring for 5 minutes. Wipe through a sieve, add the lemon zest, vanilla sugar and starch, diluted in a small amount of cold water. Stirring, bring the sauce to a boil, pour brandy, mix thoroughly and remove from heat. Cold sauce to serve to cereals, casseroles from cereals and pasta.

Berry sauce with white wine materials

Ingredients:
- 300 g strawberries
- 300 g of raspberry
- 100 grams of red and black currants
- 200 g of sugar
- 70 ml of white dessert wine

Preparation:
Berries carefully sort out, wash, remove stems and sepals, rub through a sieve. From sugar and 100 ml of water, prepare the syrup, strain. Mix the syrup with the berry puree, add wine, mix. Serve sauce in hot or cold form to desserts, puddings, casseroles.

Berry sauce with madeira

Ingredients:

- 400 g strawberries
- 200 g of raspberry
- 200 g black currant
- 350 g of sugar
- 100 ml of Madeira
- 1 teaspoon grated orange peel
- 1 packet of vanilla sugar

Preparation:

Strawberries, raspberries and black currants to sort out, wash, remove stems and sepals, add sugar, vanilla sugar, orange peel and 100 ml of water. Bring to a boil and cook over low heat with constant stirring for 5 minutes. Wipe through a sieve, add Madeira and mix. Serve the sauce with desserts and fresh fruit salads.

Berry sauce with cream

Ingredients:
- 150 g black currant
- 100 g of raspberry
- 100 g strawberries
- 150 ml cream
- 100 g of sugar
- 10 g of starch

Preparation:
Berries sort out, wash, remove stems and sepals, put in a stewpan. Add 50 ml of water and sugar, bring to a boil and rub through a sieve. In the resulting mashed potatoes add starch, diluted in a small amount of cold water, bring to a boil with constant stirring, remove the feces and cool. Add cream and whisk until smooth Serve the sauce with berry and fruit desserts.

Gooseberry sauce with wine

Ingredients:

- 400 g of gooseberries
- 100 g of sugar
- 100 ml of white wine
- 15 g of starch
- 1 packet of vanilla sugar

Preparation:

Gooseberries sorted, washed, removed stems, put in an enameled container, add 70 ml of hot water and cook on low heat until soft. Wipe berries through a sieve, add sugar, vanilla sugar and wine, bring to a boil with constant stirring. Add the starch, diluted in a small amount of cold water, again bring to a boil and remove from heat. This sauce can be served not only to sweet dishes, but also to dishes from fried poultry and game.

Sauce from gooseberries and red currants

Ingredients:
- 400 g of green gooseberries
- 200 g red currant
- 1 orange
- 150 g of sugar
- 100 ml of white wine
- 15 g of starch
- 1 packet of vanilla sugar

Preparation:
Wash the orange, grate it with the rind. Gooseberries and currants, clean, remove the pedicels, put them in an enameled container, add 70 ml of hot water and cook on low heat until soft. Wipe berries through a sieve, add orange, sugar, vanilla sugar and wine, bring to a boil with constant stirring. Add the starch, diluted in a small amount of cold water, again bring to a boil and remove from heat. Serve hot or cold.

Cranberry Sauce

Ingredients:

- 500 g of cranberry
- 250 g of sugar
- 100 ml of red wine
- 15 g of starch
- Ground cinnamon

Preparation:

Cranberries to sort out, wash, put in an enamel pot, pour 1 liter of water and cook over medium heat under the lid until soft.

Decoction to drain, drain. Berries wipe through a sieve, add a decoction, sugar and wine, bring to a boil and cook for 5-7 minutes. Add the starch, diluted in a small amount of cold water, and cinnamon, again bring to a boil and remove from heat. In hot form, serve the sauce for the fried bird, in the cold - for pancakes, fritters, casseroles.

Almond and orange sauce

Ingredients:
- 700 ml of milk
- 150 g of peeled almonds
- 200 g of sugar
- 5 egg yolks
- 2 oranges
- 30 g of butter
- 25 g of flour
- 1 packet of vanilla sugar

Preparation:
Almond should be given with boiling water, peeled and passed through a meat grinder. Add 100 g of sugar and milk, mix thoroughly and rub through a sieve. Oranges to wash, peel the grated peel, squeeze the juice out of the pulp. Egg yolks to grind with the remaining sugar, softened butter and flour. Add almond paste, orange juice, zest and vanilla sugar, cook in a water bath until thick, constantly stirring with a wooden spatula. Ready sauce to cool, serve to puddings and casseroles.

Cowberry sauce

ngredients:

- 500 g of cowberry
- 250 g of sugar
- 1 orange
- 100 ml of red wine
- 15 g of starch
- Ground cinnamon
- Ground cloves

Preparation:

Wash the orange, grate the grated zest, squeeze the juice. Cowberry pick, wash, put n an enamel pot, pour 800 ml of water and cook over medium heat under the lid until soft. Decoction to drain, drain. Berries wipe through a sieve, add broth, orange juice, zest, sugar and wine, bring to a boil and cook for 5-7 minutes. Add cinnamon and cloves, starch, diluted in a small amount of cold water, again bring o a boil and remove from heat. Serve the sauce with game and poultry.

Cherry-wine sauce

Ingredients:
- 500 g of cherry
- 200 ml of white wine
- 200 g of sugar
- 1 stick of cinnamon
- 1-2 buds of a carnation
- 1 packet of vanilla sugar
- 15 g of starch

Preparation:
Cherry wash, remove bones, fill with sugar and leave for 1-2 hours. Then add vanilla sugar, cinnamon, cloves and wine, bring to a boil and cook on low heat for 5-7 minutes, periodically mixing and removing the resulting foam. Remove the cinnamon and cloves, add the starch, diluted in a small amount of cold water, bring to a boil and remove from heat. Serve with puddings, casseroles and pasta, cheese cakes, dumplings.

Plum sweet sauce

Ingredients:
- 500 g black plum
- 200 g sugar
- 1 stick of cinnamon
- 1-2 buds of a carnation
- 50 ml of cognac

Preparation:
Wash the plum, cut it in half, remove the stone and put it in an enameled container. Add a little water, cook over low heat until soft, rub through a sieve. In the resulting puree add sugar and spices, cook over low heat with constant stirring until thick. Spices take out, add cognac to the sauce, mix thoroughly and remove from heat. Serve the sauce with desserts or meat dishes.

Peach sauce

Ingredients:
- 600 ml of peach juice with pulp
- 1 peach
- 20 ml of lemon juice
- 300 g of sugar
- 100 ml of white wine
- 1 teaspoon of starch

Preparation:
Peach wash, cut in half, remove the stone and peel. Cut the flesh into small cubes, sprinkle with lemon juice.

Peach the juice in a saucepan, add sugar, bring to a boil. Add the starch, diluted in a small amount of cold water, cook with constant stirring until thick. Add the wine and pieces of peach to the sauce, bring it back to a boil, remove from heat and cool. Serve the sauce with fruit desserts, biscuits, pancakes.

Apricot and cognac sauce

Ingredients:

- 600 g of apricots
- 100 g dried apricots
- 70 ml of cognac
- 250-300 g of sugar
- 1 packet of vanilla sugar

Preparation:

Dried apricots thoroughly, cut into small cubes, pour cognac and leave for 15 minutes. Wash apricots, cut in half, remove the stone. Put the apricots in a saucepan, pour 300 ml of water, cook a bit of softness. Decoction of the broth, apricots strain through a sieve. From apricot broth and sugar, boil the syrup, put in it apricot puree, pieces of dried apricots and vanilla sugar, bring to a boil and cook on low heat for 3-5 minutes. Serve hot or cold sauces.

Milk-almond sauce

Ingredients:
- 700 ml of milk
- 150 g of peeled almonds
- 200 g of sugar
- 5 eggs
- 1 packet of vanilla sugar

Preparation:
Almond should be given with boiling water, peeled and passed through a meat grinder. Add 100 g of sugar and milk, mix thoroughly and rub through a sieve. Eggs grind white with the remaining sugar, add almond mass and vanilla sugar, mix, cook in a water bath until thick, constantly stirring with a wooden spatula. Finished sauce to cool, serve to salads of fruits and berries, puddings and casseroles.

Vanilla sauce

ingredients:

- 300 ml of milk
- 100 g of sugar
- 2 egg yolks
- 2 bags of vanilla sugar
- 10 g of starch

Preparation:

Egg yolks to grind with sugar and starch. Add vanilla sugar and warmed milk, cook on a water bath or on low heat until thick, constantly stirring with sausage wood spatula. Finish the sauce and drain it. Serve with fruit desserts, puddings, biscuits.

Vanilla sauce with lemon zest

Ingredients:
- 300 ml of milk
- 100 g of sugar
- 2 egg yolks
- 1 packet of vanilla sugar
- 10 g of starch
- 10 g grated lemon zest

Preparation:
Egg yolks to grind with sugar and starch. Add vanilla sugar, lemon zest and heated milk, cook on a water bath until thick, constantly stirring with sausage wood spatula. Finish the sauce and drain it. Serve with fruit desserts, puddings, biscuits.

Vanilla-chocolate sauce

Ingredients:
- 300 ml of milk
- 100 g of sugar
- 2 egg yolks
- 2 bags of vanilla sugar
- 50 g of cocoa
- 10 g of starch

Preparation:
Egg yolks to grind with sugar and starch. Add cocoa and vanilla sugar, mix thoroughly. Pour a thin stream of heated milk, cook on a water bath until thick, constantly stirring with sausage wood spatula. Finish the sauce and drain it. Serve with fruit desserts, puddings, biscuits.

Vanilla sauce with nuts

Ingredients:
- 500 ml of milk
- 150 g of sugar
- 100 g of peeled walnuts
- 4 egg yolks
- 1 packet of vanilla sugar
- 10 g of starch

Preparation:
Nuts dry in the oven or fry in a pan without adding oil, crush in a mortar. Egg yolks to grind with sugar and starch. Add nuts, vanilla sugar and warmed milk, cook on a water bath or on low heat until thick, constantly stirring the sauce with a wooden spatula. Finish the sauce and drain it. Serve with fruit salads, baked goods.

Chocolate and milk sauce

Ingredients:

- 200 g chocolate with a high content of cocoa butter
- 200 ml of milk
- 1 packet of vanilla sugar

Preparation:

Chop the chocolate into small pieces, put in a saucepan, add hot milk and vanilla sugar. Warm up in a water bath with constant stirring until the chocolate dissolves. Serve the sauce with ice cream, puddings, biscuits, baked apples and pears.

Chocolate-rum sauce

Ingredients:
- 30 g of cocoa powder
- 25 g of flour
- 150 g of sugar
- 1 packet of vanilla sugar
- 40 ml of rum

Preparation:
Mix cocoa with flour and vanilla sugar, add 100 ml of cold water, mix. From sugar and 400 ml of water, boil the syrup, strain. Put the syrup on a weak fire and pour with a constant stirring mixture of cocoa. Bring to a boil, cook for 2-3 minutes, cool. Add the rum to the sauce, stir. Serve with fruit, biscuits and puddings.

Chocolate sauce with hazelnuts

ngredients:

- 200 ml of milk
- 150 g of clarified hazelnuts
- 30 g of cocoa powder
- 25 g of flour
- 150 g of sugar
- 1 packet of vanilla sugar

Preparation:

Nuts should be piped with boiling water, peeled off, dried and ground in a coffee grinder. Mix cocoa with nuts, flour and vanilla sugar, add milk, mix thoroughly. From sugar and 400 ml of water, boil the syrup, strain. Put the syrup on a weak fire and pour with a constant stirring mixture of cocoa, milk and nuts. Bring to a boil, cook for 2-3 minutes, cool. Serve in warm or cold form to baked fruit, biscuits, puddings.

Chocolate-coffee sauce

Ingredients:
- 300 ml of milk
- 2 egg yolks
- 100 g of sugar
- 50 ml of strong black coffee
- 35 g of cocoa
- 25 g of flour

Preparation:
Egg yolks grind white with sugar, add flour and cocoa, mix thoroughly. Pour a thin trickle of warm milk mixed with coffee, heated in a water bath with constant stirring until thick. Sauce to cool, serve to puddings, biscuits, casseroles from cereals and pasta.

.

Printed in Great Britain
by Amazon